My Life Before the Fire

by

Billy

My Life Before the Fire
by Billy

© 1998 William R. Mitchell

All Rights Reserved. No part of this publication may be reproduced, stored in a retrieval system or transmitted in any form or by any means, electronic, mechanical, photocopying, recording or otherwise, without the written permission of the author.

Cross Timbers Books (http://crosstimbersbooks.com)

ISBN: 978-0-6151-7784-7

Printed in the United States of America

Second Edition

For Rex, 1935-1993

Preface

We who were rural children in the Thirties had a special blessing. The dark side, which has been ably documented and lamented, was something we were hardly aware of. For us, life was elemental, poignant, hard and sweet. Because we were children, and because we were all similarly "deprived," we had little sense that life could or should be otherwise. Hard labor was neither a curse nor an "expression of the Puritan ethic" but merely a requisite for survival, the stuff life was made of. Our common circumstances gave us a sense of community no civic program could ever duplicate.

Thus we accepted need and simplicity as the normal human condition, and out of that acceptance came a peace and sufficiency that stabilized us and prepared us, unawares, for trials to come. That experience is now lost to most Americans, perhaps forever, but the need and yearning for peace, stability, and sufficiency is timeless and universal. All the more need to recreate that experience, so that we can define again what we hunger for.

So I have written *My Life Before the Fire*, an account of my childhood in rural Lincoln County, Oklahoma. I have worked to tell it in words of the child I was, to keep the tone, perspective, and psychological validity of the child. The work is not fiction, but a series of vignettes that give the sense of life of that time and place as accurately as I can.

Adults of my generation will understand at once what Billy's life was like, and will, I hope, remember the resources from which the strengths of that generation derived. Those of a later time, including the children of today, may discover these resources for their own use. They will not wish to recreate the world in which I was a boy, nor do I recommend trying; the world has changed. But I believe that just as the need and hunger are timeless, so are the means to live worthily and joyfully once the awareness of the possibility of doing so is awakened. It is this awakening I hope my little book will make possible.

William R. Mitchell

My Life Before the Fire

I have been here before, and I know where I am. I have not been here at night, though, and that is a strange, different thing. It makes the place different. I know something is wrong. I can hear it in the tone of Daddy's voice as he speaks sharply to my brothers. I can feel it in the clutch of Mama's hand on my arm. Sister is crying a little, not very loud, and Mama is trying to quiet her.

I can feel fear. I can hear the fear in the excited, hushed voices of Tom and Hudon, a fear different from mine, because they know what is wrong and I know only that the fear is there. Their fear is colored by excitement, adventure—for me it is only dread. Over every other sound I hear the howl and roar of the wind and the rattle of the heavy wooden door that Daddy has pulled shut over our heads and fastened with a bar. I have been here before, but only in the day, when the cool dim light streamed in through the opening. I have never been here with the door closed over our heads.

We have brought the lantern, and it gives us light to see. The light falls yellow on the dirt floor and the timbers that make the ceiling and walls and the flat stones that make steps leading up to the door and the clay between the timbers and between the stones. The light is full of huge shadows, some that stand still in the corners and among the shelves full of jars, some that move unexpectedly around the room as we move.

The light is strange and different, too. It is not like the lamplight in the house, which is brighter and has no fear in it. It is not like the lantern light in the feedlot either, where the cows get milked in the evening. There the light dances gaily in the open spaces and runs out to meet the trees, and besides the sky is not all dark yet. It is not like the lantern light in the barn where the horses snort in their feeding troughs and stamp in their stalls. I know that the lantern light is better than the dark, but still it is very strange and I am afraid.

There is a thing outside the door that makes the wind howl and the door rattle in its frame. It would like to come in where we are but so far it is not able. It pulls and yanks at the door, but the door will not open up though it bangs and rattles away. Daddy is afraid of it too, I can tell, but he is not afraid in the way I am because he knows how the door will keep it out.

I begin to whimper softly, not much, because along with my fear I want to know what is happening. And I am not sure whether I should cry or not. Mama says quietly to me, "Hush, now!" and I stop whimpering and listen to the wind. I can do nothing but trust that Daddy will keep the thing out and Mama will know how to hide me.

At last the wind begins to hush too. The thing has gone away howling. We listen to it for a while as the boys talk excitedly. At last Daddy unbars the door and lifts it up and stands in the hole where the door was, and Thomas and Hudon climb up beside him and look out too. "It's all over," Daddy says. Then someone brings the lantern, and Mama carries me out into the soft, dark rain.

A blackness comes down on the experience. Before it there is nothing—after it, scraps and glimpses. It is my first memory. I am not yet three years old.

Our house stands on the top of a hill. The land falls away on every side—gently to the south and west, sharply to the north and northwest and east. We live at the very south edge of our farm. Across the barbed-wire fence a few yards south of the door the pasture belongs to somebody else, and his cows graze there. I am not allowed to go across the fence and play over there, although I can go there with Mama or Daddy or one of the older kids. But I do not need to play over there. I have lots of good places to play in our own yard.

In the fringe of grass and trees between the yard and the fields that lie below it, there are hiding places, and sandy paths the cows use, and especially north of the house there is a big spot of bare sandrock that has pushed through the ground. I like to lie on the gray rock when it is warm from the sun and watch the clouds float along and listen to the crows cawing in the fields. When the summer is really hot I play under a huge mulberry tree just on the edge of the field to the northwest, where the grass is thick and green.

South and west and north the edge of the sky is near, not farther than we can walk easily when I go to the

My Life Before the Fire

fields with Mama and Daddy or sometimes go to the woods with my brothers to drive in the cows. But in the northeast the land falls away from our house for miles and miles, over fold after fold of the countryside, before it rises again gently in the far distance and is lost in the edge of the sky.

Away yonder, too far away to have any shape, are small dots of white. They are bright and glistening in the sun. I don't know what they are. They are mysterious—somehow they don't belong in the sweep of field and pasture and green woods. I am a little afraid of them. I call them "kaws" and sometimes I dream of them. I have a swing in a big tree east of our house, and often I swing for hours, looking across the fields and woods at the seam where they join the sky, and wonder what the kaws are.

Northwest from the house is a little valley full of fields, with thick woods on the other side. There are a few old apple trees in the fields, and between the fields are ridges of green weeds and grass. In the summers the fields are green and pretty with corn and cotton. In the fall they are empty and clean of all growing things, almost as bare as the gray rock that comes through the earth on the near edge, and little whirlwinds play there and kick up spirals of dust.

Sometimes in the summer evenings we go across the fields to milk the cows that come to a lot fenced in from the edge of the woods. The cows are big and friendly and I like them, but Mama doesn't want me to go over to the cows' lot by myself. She says there are "wools" in the woods. That is all she tells me about them, except that some evenings we hear a howling in the woods and Mama says they are wools.

I wonder often about the wools, and what they look like, and what they are saying to one another when they howl, and why I am not supposed to go where they are. I try to imagine what they look like. When I ask Mama what they look like she says that they are big and have big mouths and hair all over their bodies. I have dreams about the wools. I dream that I go to see the wools and sit down with them at their place in the woods, and the wools tell me all sorts of things I want to know but can't understand. I am not afraid of them, in my dreams.

On the other side of the woods there are other fields, and a canyon with water running in it all the time. I do not go there much, but in the early fall I go with Mama and Daddy when Thomas and Hudon and Mary-Margaret are in school. Mama puts some food in a bucket and covers it with a white cloth, and she carries some water in a jar too, and Daddy carries the cottonsacks and a quilt. Daddy puts me on his shoulders and we go walking much faster than I can walk through the woods past the cowlot, down a road the wagon and cultivator use and the cows walk there too as they go through the woods to where they eat.

The woods are deep and green and beautiful, with thick brush and blackjack and hickory trees and full of the sounds of birds and the locusts singing. On Daddy's shoulders I watch the woods and hear the birds and locusts and I am very happy. When we come through the woods and climb over the barbed-wire fence there is a big field of cotton ready to pick, with the white cotton like flowers all over the field.

There is a huge red oak tree at the south side of the field, on the edge of the woods, where the land slopes away down the field. I stay on the quilt in the shade of the tree and watch Mama and Daddy move slowly down the field and then after a long time come back slowly, bent over to pick the white cotton and pulling the long cotton sacks behind them. I sleep a little on the quilt in the shade, with the noise of the birds, and the crows in the distance cawing, and when I wake the flecks of sunlight dancing through the shade where I am lying, and the wind making the trees talk softly to one another.

At noon we take bread and milk and some jelly and boiled potatoes out of the bucket and the three of us eat together. I sleep again during the early afternoon. Later Mama comes dragging her cottonsack to the wagon that stands at the edge of the field and leaves it there, and then we take the bucket and the quilt I have slept on and start home through the woods as the sun is getting low in the west.

Mama cannot carry me all the way, so I must walk, but I am glad to walk through the woods, loud with bird sounds and things rustling in the brush. I find the funny doodle-bug holes in the sandy road, and the red and yellow pop-balls that grow on the underside of the blackjack oak leaves, and the patterns in the sand where terrapins and lizards have been. But we cannot stop long to look at them, because Mama must cook our supper and it will be dark after awhile. I am tired at the end of the day but I lie awake in bed, hearing the sounds of the woods in my mind and seeing the flickering sun through the trees that talk in the wind.

I sing to myself hours on end. Mama says I could hum tunes before I could talk. I cannot remember a time when I did not know many songs. Mama and Daddy have sung me songs to hush me and lull me to sleep since I was born. I can remember night after night, the singing and the rocking, and everything gone asleep except my mind, while I fight to stay awake enough to listen to the music.

Mama sings hymns for lullaby—"There Is a Fountain," "Rock of Ages," "Now the Day Is Over," "Oh Day of Rest and Gladness," "Walking in Sunlight, All of My Journey," and "I'll Fly Away, Oh Glory," and many, many more. She has a high, sweet voice that gets very soft when she thinks I am asleep.

Sometimes Daddy rocks me and sings to me too. He loves to sing "Sweet Hour of Prayer" and "Standing on the Promises" and "Loyalty to Christ," but he sings louder and his chest throbs when he sings, and besides his songs do not really lull me. He also sings "Barnacle Bill the Sailor" and "Rocked in the Cradle of the Deep" and some very sad songs like "My Sweet Kitty Wells" and "Babes in the Wood."

I cannot stand to hear "Babes in the Wood"—it always makes me cry. I begin to whimper almost as soon as the song begins, but at the lines "Those poor little babes, they lay down and died" I cry uncontrollably. Daddy does not sing that song to me after he finds out I am going to cry when I hear it, but Thomas and Hudon think it is funny that I cry at a song, so they will sing it to me sometimes just to make me cry. I try not to cry, but I cannot control my feelings. But in spite of "Babes in the Wood" I love to be sung to and I love to sing.

We have an organ that stands in the corner by the bookshelf. It is Daddy's joy. He plays the organ nearly every night after work is done and supper is over. Often he will hold me in his lap and help me press down the keys while he works the pedals. Often I will drift off to sleep hearing the chords of the organ and Daddy trying to make it play the melodies of his favorite songs. It can play some of them right, but some of them it gets wrong. I can tell where it gets them wrong.

My days are full of song. Even when I am not singing there is music in my mind. Mama sings in the kitchen at her work; Daddy sings in the fields. Mary-Margaret sings continually; even my brothers sing when they think nobody is listening. But I sing more than any. When the older ones are in school and I play for hours and hours by myself, I sing almost all the time. If I wake in the night there is a song in my mind.

It is the Christmas after my fourth birthday. We are at the Christmas music program at the one-room school where the big kids go. I am sitting with Mama and Daddy in a very large crowd of people. I am fascinated by the streamers of red and green crepe paper strung across the room, and the huge red crepe-paper bells hanging from the ceiling. But mostly I am aware of the music. I do not try to sing but only listen. The people all are singing "Joy to the World" and "It Came Upon a Midnight Clear" and "Away in a Manger."

I am hearing something strange and wonderful in "Joy to the World"—none of the songs I know are like that, with singing going on two different ways at once. It is startling, it is delightful, it is very beautiful. All the way home I hear the music in my mind. In the days that follow I try to sing the tunes, but I cannot sing them all at once. I cannot sing "and heaven and nature sing" and at the same time sing another "and heaven and nature" that starts in the middle. But I remember how it sounds.

Outside our kitchen door near the cellar where we hid from the wind is our well. Two poles stick up from the ground with another short pole across the top of them. From the pole on top a pulley is hanging with a rope that goes over the pulley, and a long metal bucket that can be let down into the well. When Mama or Daddy or the big kids let it down, the pulley creaks and grinds. Mama lets it out slow, but the boys just let the bucket fall fast, the rope running fast in their hands and the pulley creaking loud and fast and the spokes in the pulley all in a blur.

Down in the well the bucket rattles against the casing too, then it makes a throaty plop when it hits the water, and the plop and the gurgling sound echo all up the well, in a sound that is like no other sound I can remember and that I can't make though I try. Then when the gurgling stops you pull on the rope, hand over hand, and loop it on a board sticking out from the pole on the left, and the full bucket knocks on the casing and the pulley creaks slow and in a lower voice this time, and finally the metal bucket comes out of the casing. You can take the wet bucket in your right arm while you hold the rope in your left hand, and pull it out from the well and dangle it over a pail and with your thumb lift the hook at the top of the bucket, and the water will rush out sparkling and cool and clear and fill the pail. Then you must put the long bucket back inside the casing and tie the rope around the board so the bucket can't fall.

Even in the hot summer the water is cold and fresh. I am too little yet to draw water out of the well, but if I am there I always reach to touch the cold bucket while it is still wet to my hand.

One morning early I hear voices out by the well and run to look out the kitchen door. It is only once in a great while that anybody comes to our house, except for Leo that lives far over to our east where the sun shines back from his windows in the late afternoon. But this is not Leo's voice and besides there are several voices.

Daddy is standing by the well. He has tied the rope so the bucket stays up in the air, and he holds the bucket in his left arm out away from the well. Three other men are there too. One drinks from the dipper and then hands it to another who fills it from the bucket and drinks too.

They are strange-looking men. Their skin is very brown and they aren't wearing any shirts and their black hair is braided and hangs down their necks. Their faces are shaped different too.

Mama comes to the door behind me and puts her hands on my shoulders to keep me from running outside. She doesn't go out either, but stands in the door behind me with her hands firm on my shoulder.

Daddy and the men talk together for a while, though I can't tell what they are saying. Then the men give him back the dipper and go off down the hill through the fields. Daddy says something to them as they go away, and one of them turns and lifts his hand. They walk fast in a long stride, standing up straight.

Daddy comes inside and talks with Mama. I cannot understand much of what they say, but I can tell Mama is worried and Daddy is trying to assure her everything is all right. They call the men Indians. Daddy says they have a "camp" across the creek in the woods. He says they will only hunt and not bother us. I can tell that Mama is still uneasy. I think it is strange that the Indians would hunt on our place, when it belongs to us, but if Daddy doesn't care it must be all right. They can stay in the woods, like the wools, if they want to.

I don't really know what the planes are. I know that they fly around in the sky like the birds, but I don't know why. Sometimes they go straight across the sky from one side to the other, til they get as little as a speck and then I can't see them any more. But sometimes they fly round and round, and climb and dive and turn over on their backs.

The planes must be happy because they make music all the time. When they fly straight across the sky they start humming before they get near, then they hum loud and then not so loud, for a long time as they go away. When they climb or dive they have a different song, because they are happier. When they dive they sing loud at the fun they are having.

At night, if it is very dark, we can sit out in our yard and see the lights in the distance. There is a little clump of lights away to the northeast just on the edge of the sky, and a faint glow on the dark line of the earth to the southeast. But most of all I like the lights that make a long finger that sweeps across a whole corner of the sky, slow when it begins close to the ground but fast in the flash it makes across the sky before it settles slow to earth again on the other side. Then after a little bit it makes the same sweep again, over and over. Daddy says they are airplane beacons, so the planes that fly at night know where to land.

There is one of them in the southeast, where the glow is, and another in the northwest, very faint, and another far, far away to the north. They are very strange and wonderful to me, and I think it is kind of them to stay up all night to guide the planes home.

Our dog Ring is very old. He is my fiend and I like him a lot, and we play together. I talk and sing to him, and sometimes he will wag his tail and rub his head against me. But many times he will only follow at a slow trot when I try to get him to run with me, and will come slowly or not at all when I call him.

Everybody likes old Ring at our house. Daddy will often sit outside in the moonlight smoking his pipe with Ring curled up beside him and his hand laid on Ring's head. Mama puts milk and bread in a pan for him just outside the kitchen door. Sometimes when the wools howl he will whine softly and Daddy will speak to him and pat him on the head and he will hush.

One morning I am trying to get him to run with me, and he does not want to run. I coax him, "Come on, "Ring!" but he sits down and wags his tail slowly. I reach over and take the white fur on his neck in my hands and tug, trying to make him get up and run. But instead of getting up he makes a dark, heavy sound in his throat—not very loud.

I have not heard him do that before. There is something in what Ring is saying that makes me step back and listen and let go his fur. I look at him in the face and he looks back at me. It is Ring, all right, but he looks strange. But he does not say anything else and I do not know what he means. So after a few seconds I say, "Come on, Ring!" and tug on his fur again.

This time something terrible and new happens. He makes the sound again, and now it turns into a louder and frightening sound. His lips curl up and his old yellowed teeth show and he turns his head quickly and bites my arm. He just snaps quickly and lets me go at once, but there is a sharp pain and my arm is getting bloody around the marks his teeth have left. I am hurting but more than that I am scared, not of Ring only but of something else new and terrifying, something I have dreamed of sometimes, something that feels like the kaws in my dreams.

I run screaming to Mama, holding my arm, and she says "What is it?" in a scared voice and I say "Ring bit me!" and keep screaming and crying. Daddy has heard and looks at my arm and runs outside while Mama is hugging me and hushing me.

By the time I have stopped sniffling I am hearing a sound outside. I hear it over Mama's voice. It is a yelping and whining that comes from first one place and then another. I run to the door and look out and see Daddy running after Ring with a big stick. Every time he gets close enough he hits Ring with the stick, and then Ring will try to run away from him. But Ring cannot run fast or very far at a time, and finally he just hunkers down and lies still while Daddy beats him and beats him with the stick, while he yelps at every blow.

I feel strange. At first I am glad Ring is getting hurt for biting me. But his yelps are painful to hear. I feel like I feel when I hear "Babes in the Wood" and by now I am crying again, not from the pain but because Ring is being hurt and it is somehow my fault.

At last Daddy throws away the stick and walks away from Ring. Ring whines softly for a little longer but he soon quiets and crawls away under a bush. Daddy does not come back to the house but walks off toward the barn with his head bent down.

Billy

I would like to go see about Ring, but I am now afraid of him a little, and besides I think he will not want to see me. Mama talks to me and pets me and washes my arm and puts coal oil on the bitten place and wraps it in a rag and gives me some bread and milk to eat, and I feel better. But I do not feel happy all that day.

I am very sorry about what happened to Ring. I do not try to play with Ring for a long time. He does not like me any more anyway. I can tell because he looks at me differently and walks away instead of coming to me as he used to.

Sometimes I think I will go up to Ring and say I am sorry, but I never do. Ring does not do much at all, but goes to lie every day under the bush where he crawled after Daddy hit him. One day I do not see Ring any more. I hear Mama and Daddy talking about him, but I do not understand what they are saying. He is not around the house—I watch for him and even go out and look at the bush where he used to lie, but he is not there, and I never see him again.

After Ring goes away we do not have a dog for a long time. I have to play alone. Sometimes I think I'll go outside and play with Ring and then I remember he isn't there any more.

Daddy goes out in the yard in the evening, out where he always did when Old Ring used to come and lie down by his feet. He watches the beacons and smokes his pipe and doesn't say anything. Sometimes I go out there too but Daddy doesn't want to talk. I sit and watch the fire in his pipe get bright and then get dim again, and then I go back in the house.

One afternoon Thomas and Hudon come in from school a little late. They are going to high school in McLoud and have to walk from where the bus lets them off. Hudon is carrying a dog—a little white dog, with black spots. He saw her out beside the road and made the bus driver stop while he went out and got her. She is very round and her leg is hurt and Hudon has carried her all the way from where he got off the bus.

Hudon goes into the kitchen and gets some bread and milk and puts them in a pan for the dog to eat. Mama says what if she belongs to somebody and Hudon says if she did they just threw her away. When Daddy comes in from the field he looks at her and laughs a little. Daddy says she's not good for much, looks like she can't drive cows and can't tree a squirrel. Hudon gets her some more bread and milk. She is hungry.

Hudon calls her Clementine. He gets the name from a song he sings a lot. It goes "O my darlin', O my darlin', O my darlin' Clementine, Thou art lost and gone forever, dreadful sorry, Clementine."

Clementine is going to have puppies.

Away off to the north, there is a road that goes into the woods, and on over the hill where I can not see the road comes out again and then goes on over another hill to the store. The store is on another road called the highway where cars and big trucks and buses go very fast. Though the highway is far off, on quiet nights we can hear the cars and trucks go by. The trucks make loud angry noises sometimes. Daddy says that is because they have to go up a hill and it is hard work.

Every so often we have to go to the store. Sometimes someone will walk if we do not need to buy very many things, but usually Daddy or maybe Thomas will hitch the horses to the wagon and drive the wagon to the store, because we need to buy a big sack of flour or a block of salt for the cows, or feed for the cows and horses. Also we need to take the cream cans and the egg crates to the store to get money to buy the flour and feed, and the cream cans are too heavy even for Daddy to carry. Mr. Fowler will give Daddy money for the cream and eggs, and then Daddy will give Mr. Fowler the money back for the things we need.

We have to buy flour and salt and sugar and coffee and lard and feed for the animals, and sometimes we even buy crackers and soap. Mr. Fowler has lots of other things to sell, but we do not buy them. He has pop in bottles in a box with ice water in it, and cookies in a glass case, and nice white soft bread wrapped in paper. He has candy, too. Whenever I ride to the store in the wagon or walk with Mama, I always look at the cookies and candy and put my hand inside the pop box in the cold water. I can smell the bread all over the store. If we buy a lot of things, sometimes Mr. Fowler will put in a few pieces of candy and I will get some of it when we get home.

There is one other thing we buy when Daddy goes to the store. He will ask Mr. Fowler for all the other things, and then if he has some money left he will buy a little white sack of Country Gentleman smoking tobacco for his pipe. If I am with Daddy when he buys Country Gentleman, he will buy me a piece of candy too.

At night when all the cows and horses have been shut in their barns Daddy sits outside and looks at the stars and smokes his pipe. Lots of times I go out and sit with him. We do not talk very much. On dark nights the sky is full of stars, but where we are I can also see the dark line where the corner of the house is and the dark trees moving a little in the wind and the bright red spot of Daddy's pipe. In the dark the tobacco smells sweet and strong.

Daddy always carries the pipe in his overalls pocket and wooden matches in a little bib pocket all in a row with the heads sticking out so they won't get damp when his clothes get sweaty. He carries the little white sack of Country Gentleman in his hip pocket. Sometimes in the fields he stops and sits in the shade while his hoe leans against a tree or the horses stand still in their harness, and he takes out his pipe first and cleans out the bowl and knocks out the black dust he has raked loose, and then he takes out the little white sack with its yellow drawstring and pours a little tobacco out into the bowl. Sometimes he will pick up some of the tobacco from the top of the bowl with his thumb and finger and put it back into the sack carefully. When the sack gets empty he will just put the pipe in his mouth for a little while and then put it back in his pocket.

Along with the sack of Country Gentleman there is always a little packet of white papers. They are stuck on the side of the sack, under the picture of the man in a hat on the paper that goes around the sack. When he first gets the sack from Mr. Fowler, there is another piece of paper that is pasted across the top of the sack and down the side across the pack of little white papers. Daddy has to tear this paper before he can open the drawstring and get any tobacco out. He doesn't use the little white papers, so he takes them off and throws them away. Sometimes I get them and play with them.

One day I walk to the store with Hudon. He is thirteen years old and can walk very fast, and I have to hurry to catch up and get tired before we get to the store. We do not need very many groceries, but Hudon lets me carry some.

On the way home through the woods we stop to rest in the shade. Hudon takes out the sack of Country Gentleman from the bag he is carrying and turns it over and over in his hand. I am glad to sit and rest a little bit, but it is getting late and we should go on home.

Hudon holds up the sack of Country Gentleman for me to look at. "See the funny man in the hat?" he asks me.

"Yes," I laugh. The man doesn't really look funny. He looks very important in his fine hat that is not like the straw hat Daddy wears in the field, and he is smoking his pipe. There is nothing very funny in that, but I want to laugh if Hudon thinks it is funny.

"What a silly old man," Hudon says. "I wonder if we could just tear him right off of there." He acts like he is trying to tear the paper, but he doesn't. "Can you tear him off?"

I take the sack of Country Gentleman and tear the paper in two. It was not hard to do at all. Hudon grabs the sack away from me. "Oh, oh!" he says. "You shouldn't have done that. Daddy may get mad at you for tearing the paper."

That bothers me, and I think about it a lot as we walk on. I don't see what it hurts to tear the paper. Daddy is going to tear it anyway, though of course he tears it very carefully, not right across the man's face the way I did. But when the tobacco is all gone he will throw the sack away. Once he even gave me an empty sack to put my marbles in. So maybe Daddy won't care.

I have walked on ahead, but Hudon has been walking way behind me. He is doing something funny with the little white papers that go with the sack. I can not quite tell what. He has one of the papers rolled up in his hand and puts it up to his mouth. When he sees me looking at him, he turns his back to me for a moment and then throws the paper away.

When we get home, Daddy takes the sack of Country Gentleman out of the other groceries and takes out his pipe. Suddenly he stops still and looks at the sack for a long time.

"Why, the seal is broken on this sack!" he says. He turns to Hudon. "And the papers are gone. Was it this way when you bought it?"

Hudon looks scared. "Billy tore it open," he says.

Daddy looks at me, very strange. "Did you tear this sack open?"

"Yes," I say.

"Why?"

I don't quite know how to answer. "There was this funny old man on it," I say. "I tore the funny man in two."

Daddy takes me by the shoulders. "You mustn't bother Daddy's tobacco."

I am beginning to cry. I think I am going to get a spanking. Thomas and Hudon get spankings every so often, even Mary-Margaret got one once, but I have never been spanked by Daddy. Mama spanks me a little sometimes.

Sure enough, Daddy turns me around and gives me three or four spanks. They are not very hard and don't really hurt very much, but I hurt in my chest and I cry and cry. I go away outside and cry by myself. I feel the way I feel when I hear Daddy sing "The Babes in the Wood."

After awhile I hear Hudon getting a whipping too, and that makes me feel a little better. I am still crying, though. Soon Daddy comes out where I am and picks me up and hugs me. "Now, now," he says. I put my arms around his neck and stop crying, and I feel better.

At supper Hudon will not look at me. He doesn't look at me or play with me for a long, long time.

Way out through the woods to the west Daddy and the big boys are clearing new ground. That means they cut down the big trees with the crosscut saw and chop down the saplings with an axe, and dig out bushes and sprouts with a grubbing hoe. They pile up the little brush, and cut the limbs off the trees and pile them up in big brush piles. They saw up the logs from the big trees and split them for fence posts, and cut the limbs and little trees into pieces just long enough to fit in our stoves. They lean the fence posts against one another and pile all the firewood in neat little stacks they call ricks. They will haul the firewood to the house later after it is dried out.

All day the brushpiles are burning. When I go down to the new ground with Mama as she takes them lunch I see the fires burning and the blue smoke curling up, and smell the burning leaves and wood. The big stumps are burning too.

Clearing new ground is very hard work, and I am too little to help. When I get bigger though I will be able to cut with the axe and the saw too. Daddy and the boys work all day when the boys are not in school. When they come up to the house at night they are very tired. Mama and Mary-Margaret will milk the cows so the menfolks won't have to. Mama will fix a big supper of beans and biscuits and gravy and fried potatoes with onions in them, and we will have supper late, after dark.

When the new ground has no more trees or brush on it, Daddy hitches the horses to the plow and starts plowing. He plows very slow and stops often to chop at roots or move rocks out of the way. I get to play in the furrow the plow has made. The earth is dark brown and moist and crumbly, and it smells sweet and rich. Where the runner of the plow follows the share, it makes a little square wall on one side and the share throws the dirt over on the other, like turning over the pages of a book, and there is a flat bare place where the bottom of the plow runs too. You can take little sticks and build little fences in the furrow, or make a lean-to against its side. After a long time the plow will come back around, with the horses pulling slow and steady and Daddy holding the plow straight, and the share throws another layer of dirt into the old furrow where I have been playing.

When the field has been plowed Daddy lets the horses pull the harrow over it to make it smooth and drag more of the roots and twigs out of it, then it is plowed with the sweep plow to make ridges and little valleys. Then it is ready to plant. We plant potatoes and sweet corn and other garden, and I help. I can drop the seed corn in the furrow, two seeds at a time, and Mama comes behind me with a hoe and pulls dirt over them. I can put the potatoes in the furrow too. They have to be put with their eyes up. But I cannot put the tomato plants or sweet potato plants in the ground.

Every few days we go down to the new ground to watch the plants grow, and pick the potato bugs off the vines and the worms off the tomatoes. The weeds have to be hoed out or pulled up, so our crops will grow. The coons eat the corn when the ears begin to get big, and the birds peck the tomatoes, and the crows scratch up the peanuts. But they can't eat it all.

After a while we can gather food to eat. What I like best is the potatoes cooked with the jackets on. When they are peeled

Billy

you mash them on your plate with butter and salt and pepper, or you pour gravy over them. They taste like the smell of the new earth.

Almost always I play alone. My brothers and sister are too big to play with me, and besides they don't like the same kind of play. They ride the horses bareback, and hunt for squirrels and rabbits in the woods, and read their books that have no pictures in them. Besides when school starts they are gone all day long.

But I don't care. I like to play alone. I swing in the swing and watch the kaws in the distance. I make up stories and tell them to myself aloud. I sing lots of songs and even make up songs. I play like I am as big as Thomas and Hudon and I can go to school too.

No other little kids come to our place. Nobody lives close by except Leo and his folks, and they are all big people over there. There are some little kids like me that I get to see when we go to church on Sundays at the schoolhouse, but you can't play much at church.

I do have a friend though. Nobody can see him but me, and nobody else talks to him. We talk and sing together and run races. I tell him my stories and he always likes them. His name is Navy. He never comes in the house, and when other people come up where we are he goes away.

Sometimes I tell Mama or Daddy about Navy and what we did together that day. They listen very carefully and sometimes ask questions about him, but they never say anything about Navy unless I mention him first.

I don't know where Navy lives.

In the summertime we have lots of things to eat from the garden. We have tomatoes and green beans and carrots and squash and potatoes and corn and onions. There are grapes on the vines on the fence down by the barn, and later we will have apples. Along the fence rows there are sand plums, and Mama knows where to find poke greens and lambsquarter. When the field corn is still green and the ears get big and plump we have roastin' ears right out of the field. I like them best.

But when winter comes and it gets cold and snowy there won't be anything growing in the garden. The fields will be all empty, and even the squirrels and rabbits will stay in their holes. Then we can't find anything to eat. So we can things in the summer so's we'll have things to eat in the wintertime.

We don't can potaotes or sweet potaotes because if they stay dry and cool they will keep all winter. You can apples if you want to, but you can cut apples into thin pieces and let them dry in the sun and they will keep that way.

The way you can is, you pick all the things you want to save, and shell the peas and cut the corn off the cob, and wash it all real good. And you have to boil the fruit jars you are going to put them in. Then you cook the corn and stuff and put them in the jars. You put big red rubber rings around the tops of the jars, and put Mason lids on. And then you put the jars in a big pot called a cooker and put the lid on real tight and cook the jars, I don't know why.

After the jars get cooked you let them cool and then take them out and set them all in a row on the cupboard or table. At first you can see the juice inside still bubbling. But when they get cool enough you can pick them up in your hands. Then Mama carries them all down to the cellar and puts them in rows on the shelves where it is cool all the time. In the winter we can go to the cellar and get whatever we want to eat.

On canning days I mostly play outside because the house will get so hot from the cooking. Besides I am too little to help any and I am in the way. Mama doesn't want to stop and read to me because even when the jars are cooking she is shelling peas or cutting up tomatoes or something for the next canning. Daddy and the boys are off working in the fields and Mary-Margaret is picking things in the garden or washing jars. So I sing or play with Navy.

But today is a special canning day. All afternoon yesterday Daddy picked cowpeas. Early this morning Mama and Mary-Margaret begin shelling peas. Daddy goes back to the field and picks lots of ears of corn. Pretty soon a car comes up the road through the pasture south of us. It is Mr. and Mrs. Winkler and Valdora and Dolores and Verna and Geneva. They have brought tomatoes and green beans and we are all going to can together.

The big folks and the older girls all sit around in a circle and talk and shell peas and snap green beans and cut the corn off the cobs. They laugh a lot and are having a good time. I show Verna and Geneva my swing and we play on the big rocks north of the house. It is very nice to have other kids to play with. Verna and Geneva are very nice even if they are girls and I like them a lot. We take a long walk down the sandy road that goes north of our house. We are all barefooted and the sand is still cool to our feet.

Verna gets tired and goes back to the house but Geneva and I walk on down the road to where the two big cottonwood trees stand at the place the canyon begins, and on up to the fence on the hill. Our house looks far away. We turn around there and walk back. It is clouding up a little and a few big raindrops come spattering down on us. Geneva laughs and holds out her hands. "I can catch the raindrops," she says. "I can catch raindrops in my mouth." She turns her face up and opens her mouth and laughs again.

She has on a yellow dress. She has bright yellow curly hair.

When it gets real hot in the summer we have the Fourth of July. It is almost as much fun as Christmas.

On the Fouth of July nobody works in the fields, and the horses don't have to work either. Daddy gets up early and goes out before breakfast and shoots the gun into the air. It makes a big bang that echoes from the woods across the fields.

We all get up and have a big breakfast. Daddy and the boys don't hurry at the chores the way they usually do. Mama and Daddy sit at the kitchen table and drink coffee for a long time.

Thomas and Hudon have already got some firecrackers, and they can't wait to light them. They shoot some of them in the front yard and make a lot of noise, and make the dogs bark. I would like to light some firecrackers too, but I am too little. Then Daddy says, why don't you wait til dark and then you can see them flash, so the boys save the rest of the firecrackers.

Then Daddy and I go to Fowler's store. Daddy takes a gunny sack with him and we walk across the field and through the woods. It is getting hot already but the sand is not hot yet, and where the road runs through the shady woods the sand is cool all over my feet. We walk by Mr. Holder's house and he waves to us and says good morning. He has a flag with stars and stripes on it that he is hanging on his porch.

At Fowler's Daddy buys some things that Mr. Fowler puts in a paper sack. Then we all go out to Mr. Fowler's ice house. It is made of thick wood and it has a heavy wooden door with metal on the inside, and all inside the ice house has a metal lining. When Mr. Fowler opens the door the cool comes out at you, and there inside are lots of big blocks of ice. Mr. Fowler takes his ice pick and makes it go chip, chip, chip down the middle of a block of ice, until the block breaks apart into two blocks. Then he wraps one of these in a big piece of brown paper and puts it in Daddy's gunny sack.

Daddy carries the sack of ice over his shoulder and I carry the other things we have bought and we go home. Daddy walks fast with the sack and I have to hurry to keep up. But we rest several times. When we get home Daddy has a wet place on his back where the ice has melted a little.

Daddy puts the sack of ice down in a shady place in the front yard and covers it with a quilt, and we have dinner and rest a little.

Then Daddy takes the quilt away and takes the axe and starts to pound on the sack with the flat side until the block is all broken up into little pieces of ice. Mama brings the ice cream freezer with the can full of milk. Daddy puts the pieces of ice and handfuls of salt around the can in the bucket until the bucket is full and ice covers the top of the can. Mary-Margaret saves some pieces of the ice in a pan so we can have iced tea after awhile.

Then Daddy covers the top of the bucket with paper and folds a towel and puts it over the paper and starts to turn the crank. The crank goes around and makes a grinding sound with a little creak in it, and the ice scrapes on the side of the can and makes little cracking sounds, and when Daddy cranks faster all of it together speeds up.

Daddy holds the freezer down with one hand and cranks with the other. Every so often he will stop cranking and put in more ice and salt. Water starts to run out of the spout on the side of the freezer. Soon the freezer gets hard to crank. The sound changes and Daddy turns slower and slower. I have to sit on the freezer to hold it down. Finally Daddy says it is done.

Mama brings a plate and a knife and a big spoon, and Daddy takes the crank off the freezer and brushes the ice and salt from around the lid and opens up the can. The milk has turned into ice cream. He holds the can while Mama takes the dashers out and scrapes the ice cream off the dashers back into the can. They put the lid back on and pack the rest of the ice around the can and on top of it, and put paper over it and then the towel. Daddy sets the freezer in the shade of the house and puts the quilt over it. Mary-Margaret and I eat the ice cream that is still on the dashers but it is melting very fast.

Thomas and Hudon have been out hunting and they have some rabbits. They skin and clean them and Mama puts them in salt water for a little while and then cooks them for supper. We have the rabbits and gravy with new potatoes and green beans and coconut pie, and then we open up the ice cream. It is cold and hard and sweet, and we all sit in the yard and eat as much as we want.

It is getting dark and all over the country side we can hear the firecrackers going off at other houses. Somebody over northeast of us, the Frost kids maybe, have Roman candles, and we can see them go up in the sky. Thomas and Hudon shoot off their firecrackers too. The red ones make big booming sounds, and the little ones go bang with a sharp sound that makes my ears hurt. The dogs bark awhile but then they run away.

When the firecrackers are all gone Daddy opens the sack I carried home from Fowler's and there are some sparklers. Mary-Margaret and I get to hold them while they burn. Daddy tells me to hold it out away from me and not to let it go or hold it anywhere but by the wire handle. It is a funny-looking long grey stick, but when Daddy holds a match to it the stick begins to make little sparks of fire all everywhere. Mary-Margaret shows me how to make circles with the sparkler and it will leave a trail of light everywhere I move it.

Even when we go to bed there are still sounds of the firecrackers from way off on other farms, and with my eyes closed I can still the the fiery circles we have made.

Several times a year, but mostly in the summers, Cleta and Gail come out to see us in their car. Cleta and Gail are also called the Stubblefields. Sometimes Mr. Stubblefield comes, and once even Mrs. Stubblefield came. They are very old. Cleta and Gail are as old as Mama and Daddy, but they are not really old. Sometimes Daddy calls Mr. Stubblefield the landlord, but only after Mr. Stubblefield goes away.

Cleta and Gail wear white, pretty dresses and smell like soap, and they always smile and talk loud. When they come to the house Mama will stop her work and sit and talk with them. They always bring magazines they don't want any more, and I like to look at the pictures. Everybody in the family likes to read what they bring. Sometimes too they will bring a little candy in a paper sack. When they go back to the city they take potatoes and carrots and green onions and lettuce from our garden, or if we have butchered they take some meat.

Cleta and Gail drive a big black car that sinks deep in the sand on the road up to our house, and it wiggles and rocks as they come very slow over the sandrock place at the edge of our yard. The car smells hot and black, and it is so shiny you can see your face in the doors and the fenders.

Sometimes they come dressed in funny-looking trousers, like menfolk. When they come that way they do not want to sit and talk. They take their shotguns out of the back seat of the big car and go walking through the fields looking for something to shoot. When Thomas and Hudon or Daddy go hunting, they shoot squirrels or rabbits that Mama cooks for us to eat. But Cleta and Gail don't take the things they shoot home. They shoot crows and other birds and they will shoot squirrels or rabbits too, but whatever they shoot they just leave lying. I hear their big shotgun go *boom*, like thunder way off, not like the crack our rifle makes.

Once I heard Daddy talking to Mama about it. Daddy doesn't like for them to shoot the animals with shotguns. He says they just blow the rabbits to pieces and Mama says they don't eat rabbits anyway, and Daddy gets mad and says something I don't understand. Then Mama says why don't you tell them not to hunt then, and Daddy says they own our place and he can't tell them that, but they better not shoot a cow.

We are going to a party. I have never been to a party except the ones at the church. The big kids go to parties sometimes, real parties, at other folks' houses. But this time we are all going.

We go in the late afternoon. It has been a hot day but it is getting cooler now. We walk down a wide path that runs along the south side of our place. Mama calls it the lane. It is also called the section line. Mama says once cars and wagons came by here but now they have to go around another way because there is a canyon across it down in the woods and little trees have grown up where the wagons used to go.

We are going over to the Engerts' house. We can see their house from our house, and the sun shines back at us from their windows in the late afternoon. Leo comes to our place sometimes to talk to Daddy but his sister Cecelia never comes. And Mr. and Mrs. Engert don't come either because they are very old. I go to the Engerts with Mama sometimes. They live in a big house with a staircase and a big clock that ticks very slow and loud and goes "Bong, bong." Now Leo has built himself another little house beside the Engerts' house, and Iva that used to be Iva Giddings lives there too. Iva is very nice. She always smiles at me and talks to me even if there are grownups around.

We walk down the lane and cross the canyon and go on up the hill on the other side, through the cool woods with the red evening sun behind us, and come to the Engerts' place. There are already lots of people there. The Winkler girls and Joe Batt and Jim and Sammy Trent and their sister Twyla are there, and we all play hide-and-go-seek. The grownups laugh and talk to one another. There are ice cream freezers that people have brought and cakes and other good things on the tables inside.

Mr. and Mrs. Giddings come in their car. Mrs. Giddings is called Belle and she always drives. And Rose and Bill Beach come too. Bill is Iva's brother. He is a big fat man that can't walk. Rose drives their car. When she stops she comes around on the other side and opens the door. Then she picks Bill up and carries him and puts him down in a chair. Rose is big, bigger than Bill even, but it makes her puff to carry Bill and she gets red in the face.

It is noisy with everyone talking and the kids laughing and playing, and there are lots of lights in the house, and as it gets dark the men hang lanterns in the trees.

After a while we eat cake and ice cream, and then Eva Jo plays her accordion. Everyone listens and whenever she finishes a song people clap and ask her to play another one. She plays lots of songs. I like the music the accordion makes. I would rather hear Eva Jo play the accordion than play hide-and-go-seek even.

I eat all the ice cream I want, and play with the other kids some more. Then I am very tired and sleepy. I am trying to go to sleep in a chair. Finally Daddy picks me up and we start home. I go to sleep on Daddy's shoulder, hearing the sound of Eva Jo's accordion in my mind.

When I get big I am going to play the accordion like Eva Jo.

I spend hours looking at the magazines the Stubblefields bring. I like the thick yellow ones best. They are called National Geographics, I don't know why. The National Geographics smell like none of the other magazines smell. They have thick shiny pages that make a different sound when you turn them. There are lots of color pictures, pictures of animals and rivers and mountains, and houses that don't look like ours, and lots of people with real dark skin and no clothes on. Some of the people have sticks stuck through their lips and ears that hang way down where they have poked holes in them, and things hang from their ears.

Sometimes I can get Mama to sit down with me and look at the National Geographics. She can tell me what the pictures are about. Mama knows a lot. She can read what it says by the pictures and explain them to me. Someday I am going to learn to read about the pictures.

Everybody but me can read. The big kids read their schoolbooks at the kitchen table after supper is over. The lamp is in the middle of the table and they all sit around and read and write on note paper very fast. Mama will sit and read too sometimes, or maybe just do her sewing, and Daddy will read if he isn't too tired. We must all be quiet so the big kids can get their lessons done. I get a National Geographic and look at the pictures but I mustn't talk or ask Mama about the pictures until the studying is over.

Daddy has a whole case full of books over behind the organ. He and Mama will read these books while the kids study. Daddy's books don't have any pictures in them. They are very old and you have to be very careful when you read them so the pages won't come out. Sometimes if the big kids are not studying Mama and Daddy will read out of these books, but mostly I can't understand what they are saying.

Sometimes they read poems, and I like that. Even if you don't know what all the words mean, poems sound nice. Some of the poems Daddy likes are just like the songs we sing, I mean they have the same words the songs have. He reads "Flow Gently Sweet Afton" and "Drink to Me Only With Thy Nize," and you can hear the music in your head while you listen to the words. But even if you don't know the songs the poems sound like music.

There comes a time when Mama sits with me in the afternoons, and reads to me out of a book of poems, over and over. They are the best poems there are. They go like this:

> I have a little shadow
> that goes in and out with me
> And what can be the use of him
> is more than I can see

and so on. Another one starts like this:

> When I was sick and lay abed
> I had two pillows at my head.

There is a funny poem about a gingham dog and a calico cat. But the poem I want to hear over and over is about the little toy soldier that is covered with rust. It is a very nice poem but it makes me feel a little sad, I don't know why. I can't tell why the little boy never came back to play with his toys, when they are all waiting for him. Then there is Winken, Blinken, and Nod that sailed off in a wooden shoe, and the Owl and the Pussycat, that Mama teaches me how to sing.

I like the times we read these poems better than anything else that ever happened to me, unless maybe it is the singing and the organ music. Soon I can say the poems over to myself, and I tell Navy about them and say them to him too. But it is more fun to hear Mama read them.

Then Mama starts showing me which words on the page go with which sounds in the poem. There is a word on the page for every word you say. The letters in the word tell you what sound to make. That is the way the book shows you how to read. I already know what sound I am going to make, because I know the poem. So it is easy to read the poem.

One day we read a poem I have not heard before. That is harder to do, because the poem has some words I have not read before. It starts out

> Good morning, Sky,
> Good morning, Sun,
> Good morning, little things that run.

Mama has to help me with some of the words, but the two of us together figure it all out.

Sometimes I will get the book from where we keep it in its special place, and read the poems even if Mama can't stop to help me. Pretty soon I can read all the poems in the book.

I still can't read the National Geographics but I find some words in them I can read.

All that was before the fire. When the fire came, I forgot how to read.

It is fall again and the big kids are all back in school. Soon it will be Christmas time. But always before we have Chiristmas time there is a big pie supper at the school.

When we have a pie supper, everybody comes to the schoolhouse some evening, and all the kids come. Every woman and all the girls are supposed to bring a pie or a cake, all wrapped up in foil paper with pretty ribbons. Somebody will be auctioneer, like Mr. Batt maybe or one of the Winkler boys. That means the auctioneer will stand up at the front of the room where all the pies and cakes are on a table, and he'll pick up one and say "What am I bid" or "Who'll give a quarter to start this one" and some man or boy will say "fifteen cents" and somebody else will say "a quarter." When nobody else will give any more money the autioneer will say "sold" and the man pays the money and takes the pie. Then when they're all sold whoever made the pie or cake goes and eats with whoever paid the money.

I always eat some of whatever Mama baked, or some of whichever Daddy buys, or maybe a slice of Mary-Margaret's pie. But this year is different. Daddy gives me some money and I get to bid for my own pie, like Thomas and Hudon. Mama helps me count, and I bid several times but I don't have enough money and somebody bids more than me. But finally I bid all my money and nobody else bids, so I get a pie.

It is wrapped up very pretty. I wait and hold my pie and wonder if it is Twyla's or Pauline's or Geneva's or Verna's. But when all the pies are sold this old lady I don't know comes over and says I bought her pie, and we can eat now.

Everybody begins to eat. We open the pie. I am a little sad that I didn't get a pie to eat with one of the girls I know, but I begin to eat and the pie is very good. It is called butterscotch. I have not eaten butterscotch before, but I really like it. I eat two big pieces of the pie.

Mama is watching and she and the lady both ask if I haven't had enough. But the pie is good and besides I spent all my money for it and so I take another slice.

But I can't eat it all. In a little while I begin to feel sick. I don't want the rest of my pie. I go over into a corner away from everybody and lie down.

By the time we must go home I feel better. But I don't want any butterscotch pie for a long time.

I am standing close to Mama at the kitchen door, and I notice that she is getting fat. That is funny. I don't remember Mama being fat, in fact I know she didn't used to be, but now she is fat, her stomach sticks out in front great big, and I hadn't even noticed it before.

"Mama," I ask her, "why are you getting so fat?"

Mama is quiet for a while, but she is smiling a little, so I ask her again. When she finally answers me, she speaks very softly, although there is not anyone else around that might hear.

"I'm not really fat," she says. "There is a baby inside me."

Well! That is very strange. I look at her swollen belly, uncertain but impressed. There really must be something in there, all right. But a baby, that is hard to believe. I don't see how that could be. How did it get in there? How can it breathe? I think of lots of questions like that. But I do not want to ask all those questions. Something in Mama's voice keeps me from asking them out loud.

"What is it doing in there?" I ask at last.

"It's growing. It has to grow big enough to be born."

"What does that mean, be born?"

"When it gets big enough, it will come out. Then you will have a little brother or a little sister."

Billy

Mama is smiling while she says it, so I guess that is all right. I am a little worried that Mama might be hurt, with a baby growing inside her, and maybe she will be hurt when it comes out. But Mama is smiling, and she doesn't seem to be afraid. I would like to ask more questions, but already I have almost too much to think about.

"Will it hurt?" I ask her at last.

She laughs, but gives me a hug. "Maybe just a little, for just a little while. But it will be all right. Don't you worry. Run play, now."

I go away out in the yard and think it all over. I am not sure whether I should be happy about the baby or not. It is all interesting but I still feel strange about this amazing news.

I go off to the rocks north of the house and sit there a long time. I tell Navy all about it.

Every day I think about the news. I will be playing, or singing to myself, or watching the baby calf in the pen by the barn, and suddenly I will remember about it. When I go back to the house I will look at Mama's big belly with the baby inside it. Nobody else seems to be worried, though.

I tell Mary-Margaret, "Mama has a baby inside her."

She laughs when I say it. "I know, silly!" she says. She is a big girl, twelve years old. She can ride a horse, like the boys.

So I don't say anything else to anybody about the baby. After a while I do not think about it very much.

One evening Daddy tells Thomas to go get Mrs. Kelly from the farm south of ours and then go on to the Russells and call Dr. Kaylor. After a while Mrs. Kelly comes and soon after that a car drives up and it is Dr. Kaylor and Mrs. Kaylor. Something is going to happen. Mary-Margaret is finishing the dishes. She says to me, "It's time to go to bed. You're going to sleep in my room tonight."

I don't really want to go to bed yet, but it is unusual to sleep in Mary-Margaret's room and besides I don't belong where all the grown-ups are, so I go with her. We go to bed but we do not sleep. We talk and talk. Mary-Margaret is a big girl and does not often talk to me very much. But we talk about all kinds of things. Finally we talk about the baby.

"I think it's going to be born tonight," she says.

So that's why all the people are here. Mary-Margaret is excited. I ask Mary-Margaret all kinds of questions about babies, but she doesn't know about all these things either.

At last I get sleepy. The bed is cozy warm although the room is cool. I struggle to stay awake. Something important is going to happen and I don't want to miss it.

"I'm going to watch when it happens," she tells me.

After awhile there is the noise of people stirring around in the other room. We sit up and listen. We can hear Mama's voice crying out every so often, and other voices speaking to her. All of a sudden she cries out very loud.

"It's happening!" Mary-Margaret says. She jumps out of the bed and opens the door a little crack. A thin wedge of lamplight comes into the dark bedroom. I can see her bent over, looking through the opening.

"Is Mama all right?" I ask.

"Sh! They'll hear you. Stay in the bed. I'll tell you what happens."

But she doesn't. She just watches as Mama begins crying out again. Then after a little bit Mama is quiet.

Mary-Margaret pushes the door shut and runs quietly to the bed and gets in. Her feet are cold as ice.

"I got cold," she said. "Nothing has happened yet."

But soon Mama's voice starts again. Mary-Margaret jumps out and runs to the door and looks through the crack. I start to get up, but she says "Sh!" so I crawl back into the warm bed.

This time Mama doesn't stop. Her voice gets louder and higher, and the other people in the room are talking too. Then the crying stops and the other noises are more excited.

Billy

"I see it!" Mary-Margaret says. She is whispering, but I can hear what she says. In the wedge of lamplight I can see her shivering.

Soon the voices settle down and get quieter. Mary-Margaret shuts the door and runs back to the bed.

"I saw it," she said. "I heard Dr. Kaylor say it's a boy."

It's a boy. I have a little brother. And Mama is all right. I snuggle close to Mary-Margaret in the warm bed and drift into sleep.

His name is Rex and he sleeps a lot. He has lots of soft black hair and tiny fingers that will cling to your finger if you put it in his hand. He can even make his toes curl up like his fingers.

Mama spends a lot of time taking care of Rex and so we don't read together as much as we used to. And sometimes Daddy and I can't play the organ because Rex is sleeping. On Sundays when we walk through the fields and woods to church Mama doesn't go. She stays home with Rex and has our dinner ready when we come home.

Little brothers are nice to have but they are a lot of trouble.

Our horses are called Bill and Tony. They are both the color of a new penny with white all down their noses, and black tails and manes. In the sunlight the red hair on their backs and rumps shines like wet grass on a bright morning.

What they do mostly is pull the plow or cultivator. Daddy feeds them early in the morning, and then takes them to the horse-trough and lets them drink all they want. Then he puts the harness on. The harness is made of straps of leather and iron rings the leather is fastened to. It fits on their backs and fastens around their bellies. There are chains on the harness that fasten to the single-trees that pull the plow or cultivator or wagon or mowing machine. They have to have bridles on too, with bits that go in their mouths and leather straps called lines that Daddy holds while he drives the wagon, or ties together and puts around his waist when he plows.

Bill and Tony will stand still to be harnessed, but they don't like the bridles. Sometimes they try to keep Daddy or Thomas or Hudon from putting the bridles on. They won't open their mouths for the bits. Then Daddy has to put his thumb in the side of the horse's mouth and make him open his mouth so the bridle can be put on. When they come in from the field at noon or in the evening they are very glad to get rid of the bridles and harness. They will hold their heads down low to have the bridles taken off. When the bridles are off they will snort and shake and rear their heads. When the harness is off and they are free in their lot they will gallop around and snort and whinny. Then they will lie down in a sandy place and roll over and over, and get up and make their hides shudder to make the sand fall off.

On Sundays and on days when there is no work for them to do, Daddy will turn them loose to graze in the pasture with the cows. I think that is what they like the most. When it is time for them to come back to the barn to get harnessed up, they don't want to come. You can call and call, but they won't come until you rattle a feed-bucket, or sometimes you have to take a bucket of feed to the pasture and then maybe they will let you lead them home.

Bill is worse than Tony. He doesn't want to be caught, and if he gets loose he will run away. So Bill has to wear a long rope around his neck all the time. Once you get hold of his rope, he will go with you anywhere you lead him. Tony will not run away unless Bill does. He will follow Bill wherever Bill goes. When you lead Bill home Tony will come too.

After awhile it is so much trouble to catch Bill that Daddy won't let him go to the pasture any more. Tony can go to pasture but Bill has to stay in the lot with his rope on. Morning and evening Daddy or the boys will bring him an armful of fresh Johnson grass, and he gets plenty of hay and corn.

Or when somebody has the time, Bill gets to come out of his lot, with his rope on his neck, and go graze while somebody holds his rope. Usually he will graze not in the pasture but on the terraces between the fields, where there is lots of fresh grass that hasn't been grazed. Bill would like to graze in the corn or oats in the field, but he will not pull away if somebody holds his rope.

This afternoon Mary-Margaret has to graze Bill. She takes a book to read and I go with her. We take Bill down to the pond in the pasture this time. There is green grass on the pond dam that the cows graze sometimes but there is enough grass there for Bill too. There is a big block of salt nearby he can lick on, and he can drink from the pond if he wants to.

Mary-Margaret holds the rope and reads her book in the shade of a big cottonwood tree. I sit on the pond bank and watch the water-bugs with their long legs run back and forth on top of the water, and the big dragonflies flutter and flutter above the water, and dart back and forth and settle on a weed or stick at the pond edge. Lots of little frogs are swimming close to the bank too, with just their noses sticking out. Once in a while when Bill gets too close to one of them a big bullfrog will jump from the pond dam where you couldn't even see him, and go plop in the water like a rock you'd thrown in.

It is cool and quiet by the pond and the grass is soft where it has been grazed close by the cows. I shut my eyes but can still feel the flecks of sunlight between the fluttering leaves of the big cottonwood. I am about to drop into a nap when I feel Bill's nose rooting against me.

I wake up scared. There is Bill right in front of me, looking straight down into my face with his big eyes. He has stopped chewing the grass he has cropped and just looks at me. I can feel the breath come out of his big nostrils and his big flabby lips hang down almost in my face.

I sit up and look at him, but he still doesn't move. And then I see. A big horsefly is settled on his face. I raise my hand and swat the fly. It leaves a little bloody place where it has bit Bill's nose.

Then Bill turns and starts grazing again.

Down below the pond there is another big tree and then a low place where the water stands in the grass when it rains, and then a ditch begins. It is little at first but gets bigger and bigger until it opens up into a canyon at the place where it crosses the fence.

Right where the ditch begins Daddy has made a hotbed. He has dug a hole into the bank of the ditch, and put a steel oil drum on its side in the hole. The open end of the drum is facing the ditch, like a cave. There is dirt on top of the drum. When the weather begins to get warm just a little, Daddy brings leaves and stick and limbs and makes a fire in the drum. So the dirt on the top of the drum gets warm. Every day he will make a little fire in the drum so the earth stays warm.

In the warm earth Daddy plants sweet potatoes. If the ground is dry he will carry water from the pond and water the little plot of ground. Soon there will be sweet potato plants coming up. When the weather is warm enough, he stops making a fire in the drum. Then we take up the sweet potato plants carefully and set them out in rows in the field.

Every Sunday morning we go to church. Everybody puts on clean clothes and we walk together. We go across the fence into the pasture and down the sandy road past the fields and through the pear orchard til we come to Mr. Tucker's fence. Then we can either climb over his steel gate and go on through his pasture to his big yellow house where the mailboxes are, or we can turn east and cross the big canyon and come out on the road that goes by the Knoxes' place. Either way we get to the mailboxes, but if it is raining or muddy we don't go across the canyon.

From where the mailboxes are we go south, under the telephone wires that sing together in the wind, and then in a little while we come to the schoolhouse. That is where church is, but only on Sunday. Other days it is just school.

Most of the way Daddy will carry me on his shoulders because it is a long way and I walk too slow. Sometimes Thomas or Hudon will carry me for a little ways, but they don't really like to and besides I am too heavy for them to carry all the way.

Most of the people at church walk but some people have cars. We don't have a car.

At church somebody will play the piano, usually Mrs. Batt, and everybody will sing. I can't read the songs in the songbook but I know most of them anyway. When we have sung some songs, Mr. Winkler or Mr. Batt or Mr. Reust will say a prayer out loud and then we will sing again. I like the singing best.

After awhile the singing is over and then somebody will preach. When you preach you stand up at the front and talk to everybody real loud for a long time. Sometimes somebody will say "Amen!" but mostly everybody just listens. I don't know what the preaching is about. I can't understand it so I turn the pages of the hymnbook and see if I can read some of the words.

Sometimes I just sit and watch the sun coming in the high windows. After a long time the preacher will stop and we will sing again. Then everyone talks to everyone else for a while. I can talk to Joe Batt and Jimmy and Sammy Trent and the Winkler girls, and sometimes Buster Bridges will come with his daddy from town. Then people will begin to leave, the cars will start up, and then we will go too. Nobody goes our way but sometimes Valdora Winkler will walk home with Mary-Margaret and stay the afternoon.

I like to go to church but it is a long way home afterwards. I am always hungry when we get there. In the summertime we will have fried chicken, and lots of times we will have rabbit or squirrel if Daddy or the boys have gone hunting on Saturday. Everybody eats a big dinner, then we all rest and I will usually have a nap.

Daddy and the boys will do chores early, and then we walk back to church in the evening. It is very nice going back when it is cooler. Off to the west I can see the sun going down through the trees, and the sky turns all red, and the trees go up and down against the red sky as Daddy walks. It is nice and cool now and the locusts are singing in the woods and way off you can hear whippoorwills and turtle doves and an old crow cawing.

Billy

At the church the lamps will burn very white and bright, not like our yellow lamplight at home, and there will be a lot of singing again. The songs sound different with the bright lamps burning and the red sky in the west still showing through the windows, and the sky slowly turning black while we sing.

When church is over we walk home in the dark. We can barely see where the road goes by the trees standing up against the sky, moving their black shapes in the wind, but we know the way. I am sleepy, but I hold on tight as I ride on Daddy's shoulders. Since it is dark we do not go through the canyon but turn at the mailboxes and go through Mr. Tucker's pasture, past the windmill that creaks in the wind and the sound of the water running into the cattle-tank, and we go by the cowlot where his cows are all huddled lying down, and then through his woods with the owls hooting and the whippoorwills saying "chip flew out-of-the white oak!" Daddy opens the gate and we go through and then he closes it, and I hear the chain that fastens it clink in the dark.

Then we walk past the pear trees and then out into the open fields where there is nothing but the dark and the stars so thick in the sky they almost touch, and the milky way stretching from one corner of the sky to the other. But way off to the north where the north star is, there is a big tree you can see standing up against the sky, and that is the way we are going. Daddy holds my feet and I am holding onto his head even though I am very drowsy. I hear the whippoorwills and the owls and the sounds of the songs we sang still in my mind, and Mama humming the music to herself, and the boys and Mary-Margaret talking and laughing, and the stars rise and fall, rise and fall, as Daddy walks through the dark.

It is going to be Christmas again, and Santa Claus will come. He always comes by the church when we have our Christmas program, and he brings a sack of oranges and apples and nuts and candy for everybody, and I get one of my very own. Santa gives it to me himself. He knows me, and calls me by name. But he knows everybody else too, Thomas and Hudon and Mary-Margaret and all the grown-ups, and even the Effinger boys that wear old clothes to church and still go barefoot when it is cold.

But Santa also comes to our house on Christmas eve, and he goes to Joe's house too, and to the Trents and most everywhere, except to the Effingers maybe. He comes while we are asleep and if you hang up your stocking he will put something nice in it for you to find on Christmas morning. He brings the Winkler girls dolls, and the Trent boys get toy cars that look like their daddy's car, and Joe gets a tractor like his daddy has too. Santa has not brought me a car or tractor but I get something nice, like new socks maybe.

Joe says you can write Santa a letter, or see him in town, and tell him what you want, and if you've been good, he will bring you what you ask for. But we don't go to town and I can't write a letter yet. I ask Mama how I could tell Santa what to bring me. Mama says lots of times Santa just knows what little kids want, and he will bring it anyway, except if he has already given that present to some other little kid that needs it worse then he will give you something else that's very nice, and really you wanted it just as much as what you asked for but hadn't thought to ask for it.

But I know what I want Santa to bring me. I want a pocket knife. I tell Mama that I know Santa is going to bring me a pocket knife this year, because he knows what I want and I would like to have a knife for my own. I could whittle with it or play mumbly peg like the big boys do at church, or maybe just carry it around in my pocket, and I want to show it to Navy.

Mama says yes it would be nice to have a pocket knife but sometimes little boys cut themselves when they whittle and besides you can lose a knife very easy and then it's gone. And maybe Santa knows that and he would maybe give me something that would be a better present.

I talk to Navy about the pocket knife, and we both think Santa couldn't find any better present. So I know he is going to give me a pocket knife. I tell everybody at our house that I am going to get a pocket knife. I know Santa will give the best present, and that's the best present. I wonder if it will have a red handle.

Finally it is Christmas and I run into the living room to see what is in my stocking. We have all put our stockings up behind the heater stove. Mine is hanging on a nail down low where I can reach it. It looks empty, and for a moment I wonder if Santa forgot me. But when I take it down, sure enough there is something heavy down in the toe. I reach down and pull out a pocket knife with paper wrapped around it. The paper is a letter.

It is a real pocket knife, all right, but it isn't new. It doesn't have a red handle. The handle is a yellow kind of bone, and one side of it is broken. It has two blades, but they are not shiny bright and I can't open them by myself. I don't know how to feel about my pocket knife. I am proud and glad that Santa gave me what I wanted, but it doesn't look like I thought it would.

Mama and Daddy are right there to watch, and they want to look at the knife. I let Daddy open the blades for me. It has a big blade on one end and a little blade on the other end. Daddy says I will have to be careful with it because it is sharp. Mama opens the letter and says let's see what Santa said. She reads the letter to me from Santa, and it explains everything. Santa says he has already given all the pocket knives to other little boys, so he is giving me his very own pocket knife. And would I take good care of it because it is very special and has been all over the world.

Well! That is something! I am really proud of my knife. Joe has a red tractor but *I* have Santa Claus's own knife. I'll bet nobody else has a present like that.

I try to whittle with my knife. Daddy watches me carefully so I won't cut myself. But I can't whittle very well. Daddy says not to worry, I will get bigger soon and then I will be strong enough to whittle.

Every once in a while Daddy asks if he can borrow my knife. He always gives it back as soon as he is through with it. But one day he asks to borrow it, and I don't have it in my pocket, and I don't know where it is. I look all over the house, under my bed, out by the kitchen steps, out by the well, everywhere I have been that I can remember. But I can't find my knife.

I have lost Santa Claus's knife, the only one in the world. Daddy is sad like me, but he says I should keep looking and maybe I will find it. All day I am sad. I cry a little whenever I think about the knife. I talk to Navy about it, but Navy doesn't know where to look either.

Billy

After supper Daddy takes me to the organ and we play some songs, but it doesn't help very much. Before I go to bed I look all over the house one more time, but I can't find it.

I wonder if Santa Claus knows I lost his knife. I wonder what he will think of me, that the gave me his own knife and I couldn't keep from losing it. I feel like I feel when I hear "Babes in the Wood."

Next morning after breakfast before Daddy goes to the field he takes me on his knee. Then he takes something out of his pocket. It is the knife! Daddy found my knife. I am so glad I hug his neck. We talk about the knife, and how I was so glad to get it, and how bad I felt when I lost it, and how glad we are that it is found. Daddy thinks maybe I would like for *him* to carry the knife in his pocket so it won't get lost again. And then when I need to whittle with it I can get it from him. I think that is the best way too. I don't want to lose my knife again.

Mr. Holder lives on the place north of us. We have to go by his place on the way to Fowler's store. He is tall and thin and very old. When anybody asks him how old he is, he stands up straight and says, "I was born in sixty-one, the year the war broke out."

Mr. and Mrs. Holder have a big old house with two chimneys and a big porch on the south side and lots of barns. And roses and honeysuckle all around the house, and three cats. When I walk with Mama to the store we stop by the Holders to visit. I like to go in the Holders' house. Mama and Mrs. Holder talk and talk, and I sit and look at all the things in the house. There are lots of little shelves all over the walls, and lots of pictures of old people, and little china things and little dolls all over the shelves.

Mr. Holder has an orchard with pear trees. We don't have any pear trees, or anything but apple trees and some grape vines.

One day Mr. Holder comes to our door. He is standing in our doorway with a bushel basket on his shoulder. Daddy is very surprised to see him and asks him to come in and helps him put the basket down on the floor. It is full of big yellow pears.

Billy

Daddy says Mr. Holder shouldn't have carried a bushel of pears nearly a mile in this heat, and Mr. Holder says he had to rest once or twice. Mama and Daddy both say what nice pears they are and look at one another kind of funny, and Mr. Holder just sits and smiles and wipes his face with his red handkerchief. There are little drops of sweat all over his forehead and on his mustache and he laughs and talks in his high quiet voice. Daddy tries to give him a dollar but he laughs and won't take the money.

Mama takes the waterbucket and draws some fresh water from the well and gives him a big glass of water. Mr. Holder drinks the whole glass and says it is nice and cool and could he have another.

I am sitting in the floor by the basket, holding this big pear in both hands. It is bigger than three of our apples and besides there are no brown spots on it, and it is a bright yellow color and smells sweet. Mr. Holder says to me, "Do you like the pears?" and I say yes, and he holds his thin face up high and says "Good!"

Then he stands up and gives the glass back to Mama and says he has to be going. Daddy gets up and goes out the door with Mr. Holder. Out in the yard I see them shaking hands.

Mr. and Mrs. Holder don't go to our church. They have a car and their grown son Elmer drives them in to McLoud for church. Daddy says they are Pennycostals. That means they don't believe in using doctors.

One day Elmer comes to see Daddy. He says Mrs. Holder was hoeing her garden and was bitten by a snake, a copperhead. And she won't go to the doctor and Elmer is afraid she will die and would Daddy please come and talk to her and make her go.

Daddy goes with Elmer at once, walking fast down across the fields. He is gone a long time, but late in the afternoon he comes home. Mama asks if Mrs. Holder went to the doctor, and Daddy says no.

"She wouldn't go, and Gus wouldn't make her. I tried to talk to her, but she said, 'Now Tom, I know you mean well, but this is up to the Lord. I've lived a long, good life and if the Lord wants me I'm ready, and if he thinks it's not time yet, I'll get well.' And I couldn't say anything more."

The next day Mrs. Holder went out and hoed her garden.

Mostly the cows eat out in the pasture. They just walk around and eat the grass right off the ground. But when we have new baby calves they don't eat grass, they suck milk from their mamas. There is always plenty of milk so that we can have milk too after the calves get through.

There is a baby calf that Daddy has shut up in a pen with a shed in it, down east of our house. It stays there by itself and doesn't go to the pasture to eat with the other cows and calves any more. Daddy says we want it to eat better and get big and fat.

Every morning and evening Thomas or Hudon takes a bucket of milk for the calf. He puts his head down in the bucket and snorts while he drinks, and then he looks up at you with his ears stuck straight out from his head and milk all over his pink nose. Later when he learns to eat hay he gets some hay in a trough and some feed from the store.

I go down to the pen and talk to Calf several times every day. Sometimes Navy and I both go. Calf doesn't talk but he listens to us. When the weather is colder and I wear my coat and cap to play outside, I can see the steam Calf makes when he breathes. If I laugh at him suddenly he will jump backwards and kick his heels and snort and flip his tail while he runs around the pen. I think that is funny, but Daddy doesn't want me to make him run.

Calf gets bigger and bigger. Soon his back is higher than my head, except that when I climb up on the rails of his pen I am still higher that he is. Now he doesn't run much anymore and he doesn't sound like a baby calf when he moos.

After the weather gets real cold and I don't play outside any more and the water freezes on the well rope, I don't go see Calf much, only sometimes if I wrap up real warm I can go along when Calf gets fed and watch him eat for a little while. Calf doesn't get cold because he has a lot of red hair and he has a shed to lie in when it is cold or when he sleeps.

It is a very cold morning. I can see the ice on the inside of the windows. I take my clothes and run into the living room or kitchen and put on my clothes close to the stove, because it is too cold to get dressed in the bedroom. This morning Daddy has already been out to do his morning chores when I get up. At breakfast we have hot oatmeal with lots of toasted bread and milk. Daddy tells the boys to move the big black washpot down by the pen. I see them later carrying it down the hill. Thomas is holding it on one side and Hudon on the other. Then they carry buckets of water from the well down the hill also. Down by Calf's pen Daddy is making a fire.

Something is going to happen and I don't know what it is. I ask Mama what Daddy and the boys are doing, but she doesn't answer me. She is very busy too, getting out pots and pans and knives and fruit jars. It's like we were going to can tomatoes, or beans, but it is winter time and beans and tomatoes don't grow in the winter.

Mama tells Mary-Margaret to read to me. That is fun. Mary-Margaret doesn't usually read to me. I love to have people read to me. So we crawl into the space behind the stove where it is always warm and she reads me stories for the longest time. I forget all about what is happening outside.

Billy

Pretty soon though I hear the boys come in and go back out and feel the cold air when they open the door. They are bringing something inside to Mama and I want to go see, but Mary-Margaret says no, let's read some more, let's read about the gingerbread man, so we read. I like the story about how the gingerbread man ran away and got eaten up.

Mama is cooking something that smells very good. From time to time she puts jars on the stove and lets them boil in a big pan of water.

Then after awhile Daddy and the boys come in and they all wash their hands for a long time and then Mary-Margaret and I crawl out from behind the stove and we all eat dinner. Dinner is very good today. We have plenty of fried meat and bread, and we all eat plenty.

Then I go take my afternoon nap. It is no longer really cold in the bedroom, but it is colder than the rest of the house. I take off my shoes but sleep in the rest of my clothes, under a warm quilt.

When I wake up there is nobody in the house. Mama and Mary-Margaret must be outside helping Daddy and the boys. I get up and go into the kitchen. There are a lot of jars sitting up on the cabinet and the smell of cooked meat everywhere. There is a big pot on the stove but the fire in the cookstove is almost out and the kitchen is cooler now.

I remember that there has been something different happening. The big pot is part of it somehow. I am too little to see in the pot, but I think it has something to do with what everybody is doing.

I push a chair over by the stove and crawl up in it. On the chair I am tall enough to look into the pot.

There is something big and white in the pot. It has been cooking but now it is just getting cool. I look at it a long time.

It is a piece of the Calf. All the red hair is gone and there is just white skin. It is whiter even than my skin. But still I see by the shape of it that it is part of the Calf's leg.

I climb down and push the chair back where it was. I have seen something Mama didn't want me to see. I feel very bad. I want to cry but I can't. Also I feel afraid. I feel weak and sick and I don't want to see anybody. I go back in the bedroom and lie down and pull the quilt up around me. I am cold.

After a long time I hear Mama come in. She puts wood in the stove and I can tell by the sounds she is getting ready to fix supper. Then everybody comes in and goes out with milk buckets and feed buckets and I know the chores are getting done.

Mama comes into the bedroom and says, "Billy, wake up now, it's time to eat supper pretty soon." So I get up and put my shoes on. But I don't feel good. At suppertime I don't want to eat anything. I am not hungry. I feel a little sick. Mama is worried about me. Daddy wants to sit down at the organ with me and let me play some music, but I don't want to. I cry a little. Everybody asks me what is the matter, but I can't tell.

It is several days before I go outside again. But finally there is a warm day and I go out. I play in my swing a little and look at the kaws. It makes me feel strange to look at them. Then I go down to the pen where Calf was.

Calf is not there. The pen is empty and quiet and the gate is open. There is a black place on the ground where the fire was and some ashes. There are also some clumps of red hair. I can see where the water was dumped out of the big pot.

I do not like to be down here. It makes me feel bad. I feel worse than I do when I hear "Babes in the Wood." I go to look for Navy out where I usually find him, out by the sandrock. But he isn't there. I wait for him a long time, but he never comes.

It is the middle of the night and I have been sound asleep but now Mama is shaking me and telling me to wake up. She is putting my shoes on but she does not tie them. She speaks to me very calm and comforting, but she is in a hurry and I know from her voice there is something wrong. Mary-Margaret is there too, and Mama has the baby, and Mary-Margaret holds my hand and we all hurry out into the living room. Daddy is yelling at Thomas and Hudon to get up. There is another noise too, a loud rushing crackling noise, and the living room is lit up with a flickering yellow light, the color of sheet lightening far off in the clouds on a dark night.

Thomas and Hudon come stumbling and hurrying out of their room. Thomas has his shoes in his hands. Daddy is rushing us all toward the front door.

Mary-Margaret is pulling me along by the hand and Mama is behind us saying "Hurry, now" and she has Rex in her arms all wrapped up in a blanket. Hudon is behind Mama, and then Thomas and Daddy are last. They pick up the trunk that sits in the living room and bring it with them. Behind them the noise is louder and the wallpaper begins to peel itself off the wall and curl up in funny little burning strips and the house is full of smoke and everything is on fire.

My Life Before the Fire

We go out of the front door and on out east of the house, Thomas and Daddy last, carrying the trunk between them. They set it down by my swing in the big mulberry tree and Thomas starts back toward the house, but Daddy says no, it's too late. We all stand huddled together by my swing and watch the house. Light is coming out of every window and the roof begins to smoke and then bursts into fire. It is very hot. We have to back up farther away from the house because the house feels like a stove on a cold winter day. Up in the smoke there are pieces of burning things, and big columns of sparks reach up where the fire has gone through the roof.

It is a cold night, but I am not cold because the fire is warming me. All around us the trees are lit up with a dancing yellow light. The cedar tree that stands by the front porch is on fire now too. I can see right through the walls of our house. The boards in the walls stand up straight and black in the fire.

Mary-Margaret is crying and Mama is trying to comfort her. I do not cry. What is happening is terrible and I know it is very bad for our house to burn, but it is so strange and I want to see it all happen. I watch as the roof begins to sink down, sink down, and the boards that stood up straight begin to lean and curl over, and then the whole house falls down slowly in a big heap, still burning, burning.

We are all here.

Across the field south of us there is a car coming, its lights bouncing, bouncing, like it is really in a hurry. It comes up to the gate and stops, and a man gets out slowly and leaves the door open then he crawls through the wire gate and starts to run toward the house.

Daddy yells at him and starts toward where he is. The man turns as he hears Daddy and then runs to meet him. They talk excitedly and come down where we are. It is Paul, he is the Winkler girls' big brother. He is very glad to see us.

"I thought you were all dead," he says. "I saw it burning from over at our place. When I came up and saw that house burning, I thought you were all dead." He says it over and over.

The house has nearly all burned up now, but there is a huge red pile of coals and still some flames. The cedar tree is still on fire but it is going out. On the other side of the house the poles that hold the well-bucket are on fire. There is a big bright moon in the east.

Soon another car comes, and Leo comes running up on foot from his place half a mile east, and everybody talks and talks. Then Paul takes Mama and Mary-Margaret and me and Rex in his car. Daddy and the boys stay.

We go jouncing over the road through the field, back the way Paul came, to the Winklers' house. The car is warm inside and the motor gets louder then softer as Paul drives through Mr. Tucker's pear orchard and stops to open the gate. I am drowsy and slowly I go to sleep. We stop again at another gate, and I wake up a moment, then sleep again. The car makes a great bump as we cross a bridge and the boards of the bridge rattle and I wake up again. I sit up in the seat, and the moon is looking right in at me through the windshield. On either side of the bright moon there are dark lines of trees standing. The road is going up a hill right into the sky where the moon is.

I wake up in a strange house. At first I don't know where I am. Then I remember the fire. Our house has burned down and we have gone to the Winklers' house with Paul. It is bright outside and I am hungry. Nobody is in the room with me but I hear Mama and Mrs. Winkler talking in another room.

I climb down from the bed and go out in my underwear. Mama is holding Rex. She motions me to her while she is talking and I go to her. Mrs. Winkler smiles but I am trying to hide behind Mama. I am a little ashamed not to have clothes on. But my clothes have all burned up.

"We could put you in one of the girls' dresses," Mrs. Winkler says. "I don't have any little boys any more." She is laughing a little now but I don't think it is funny. I don't want to wear a dress. I shake my head.

Mama says, "You can wear a towel maybe." That doesn't sound very good either. But Mrs. Winkler gets a towel and Mama folds it and pins it around me like one of Rex's diapers. I feel silly wearing a diaper when I'm all grown up, but it is better than a dress.

Geneva and Verna come running into the room. They have already been outside playing. They stop and look at me and start laughing at my diaper. I try to hide from them, but Mama gives me a little push and says, "Go play outside for a little while and then we'll get you some breakfast."

So I go with Geneva and Verna, and we look at the baby kittens and then go down to the barn where the baby chickens are that make a clatter of cheeping noise, and the Winklers' old dog sniffs at me and wags his tail. Soon everything is all right.

After breakfast we get in the car, Mama and Rex and me, and the girls and Mrs. Winkler go along, and Paul takes us back to our place.

In the daylight everything looks different. You can see right through where the house was to the fields and the woods that used to be on the other side. There is the smell of burned wood and paper, and ashes and black pieces of wood and a little bit of smoke here and there. The big sandrocks that the house used to sit on are still there, with black smudges on the red rock. Where the organ used to be there is a heap of ashes and some bright metal pieces that glint in the sunshine. The old cedar tree is all burned on the side where the house was, and the frame of the well has partly burned and fallen down and the pulley is lying on the ground.

It all looks strange and sad, but at the same time it is interesting. The girls are talking excitedly and are about to walk into the place where the house was, but Paul tells them not to. Daddy comes up carrying a lump that looks like glass but it is cloudy-looking and you can't see through it. He gives it to Paul. "It was a fruit jar," he says.

Down by the big tree where my swing is there is a tent that someone has brought. We are going to live there, Daddy says, until another house can be built. He is telling Paul about it, that he walked to Fowler's store this morning and talked to Mr. Stubblefield on the telephone, and Mr. Stubblefield says we will build a new house. He will buy the lumber and stuff if Daddy will get his neighbors to help build it.

The girls and I go to look at the tent. It is nice inside and there are some cots to sleep on. Daddy says when the cook stove gets cool enough to move we will put the stove under the tree to cook on. Daddy has got the well bucket out of the well and tied another rope to it, so we can lower it into the well and have water.

Thomas and Hudon are staying with the Trents. Mary-Margaret is at the Phillipses' house. But everyone will be back soon.

Everything is going to be all right.

Today it is very cold in the tent, and the wind is blowing and blowing and making it flap and pop. That is what woke me up. I snuggle down in the covers on my cot and try to stay warm. Nobody else is in the tent.

I am so cold I want to put my clothes on. I hop out and grab them quickly and then get back under the covers. I finally get my shirt and trousers and socks on but still lie there with the covers over me, shaking.

The clothes have been brought to us by the neighbors, people that come to the church, or people that have kids in school with Mary-Margaret or the boys. I am very glad to have clothes. I don't have to wear a towel anymore, and besides it is too cold today to wear a towel.

I put on my shoes and Mama comes into the tent. She has cooked some breakfast on the stove outside and brings me a bowl of oatmeal and some bread toasted in a skillet. After we eat she fixes another bowl of oatmeal and some more bread to take to Mary-Margaret.

Mary-Margaret is sick and we don't want to catch whatever she has, so she is not sleeping in the tent. She has a bed in the corn crib, down west of where the house used to be. I put on my new coat and cap and Mama and I go down to the corn crib to take her breakfast.

The corn crib is made out of logs with clay packed between the logs, and there is a lot of corn in it with the shucks still on. The corn is dusty and the dusty smell is all in the building. Mary-Margaret has a bed of quilts in the corn. The corn crib is warmer than the tent but it is still cold and when you shut the door it is nearly dark.

We leave her breakfast and Mama says we shouldn't stay long because we mustn't get sick. Mama goes back to the tent and I play around the yard for a little while. I can walk around inside the house foundation now, if I am careful not to walk on anything that would hurt my feet. I find where the organ used to be and pick up several of the little metal reeds, all twisted from the fire. Where the kitchen was there are globs of glass melted down into strange shapes. The iron bedsteads are still in the places where the bedrooms were but they are all twisted and sunk down and the bedsprings are lying on the ground all curled up.

I go out to the sandrock, but Navy isn't there. I guess the fire scared him. I don't know whether he ever will come back.

Our new house will be in a different place. It is not going to be up on top of the hill were we can see for miles and miles, and see the kaws. Daddy has found a clearing over in the woods where he says there used to be a house and there is an old well there. It is closer to the store and there are big trees all around and it is a very nice place. But the well is just a hole in the ground.

Big trucks come and haul a lot of boards and shingles and nails and stuff to the clearing. Daddy and the big boys have been hauling big rocks to the clearing in the wagon. There are no cedar trees over there but there are some big oak trees that will be in the front yard of our new house when it is built.

One day all the men come from everywhere, and Mr. Winkler tells everybody what to do because he builds houses all the time, and lots of men start building the house. There are so many men working that the house goes very fast. By noontime there is already a floor made of clean white boards, and other men are nailing boards together to make the sides of the house, and there is the sound of hammers pounding and handsaws making their noise, and lots of men talking and laughing. Tom and Hudon help too, and the big Trent boys and Lloyd Reust. But I mustn't run and jump on the new floor or stand and watch the men making the walls, because I am just a little boy and I am in the way.

Mama and Mrs. Winkler and Mrs. Batt and all the other women cook and cook over where the old house was, and then they all carry the food in buckets and dishpans over where the men are working. They have to carry water too because the well in the clearing won't give us water yet. When the food is all there all the men stop hammering and sawing and all stand around and Daddy says the blessing just like we do at home, but he sounds different and says different words and Mama is crying.

Then everybody eats from the bowls and plates, just sitting on the ground or on the new floor or leaning against the trees. I get a sandwich made with store-bought white bread and it is very good. There are not many kids around but the Winkler girls are there and Joe Batt and Jim Trent. We have a good time. But right away the men start working again and the womenfolks gather up the dishes and the food that is left. I help Mama take stuff back to our tent where it will get washed and Mary-Margaret carries Rex. I am getting tired and when we get back to the tent I take a nap.

When I wake up and go outside I can see the roof of the new house stick up out of the trees, way off where the clearing is, and men crawling all over it nailing with their hammers. As the sun gets lower and it gets cooler there are not so many men on the roof, but we can still hear the hammers way off.

Finally when it is almost dark Mama and I walk over to the clearing. The men are all packing up their tools and going home. There in the clearing is our new house.

It has a roof and windows and steps made of rocks cemented together and a chimney and everything. It isn't painted yet and on the inside you can still see some of the boards of the frame. But Daddy says that's all right, we can finish it while we live in it.

Billy

We all walk back to our tent through the woods. I ride on Daddy's shoulders and watch the trees go up and down against the evening sky. There are birds singing and the first flowers are showing in the grasses in the meadow and a pair of cottontail rabbits gallop down the path in front of us and then jump sideways and are gone. I am getting hungry again and a little sleepy, but I am happy. We have a new home.

The End

www.ingramcontent.com/pod-product-compliance
Lightning Source LLC
Chambersburg PA
CBHW051710040426
42446CB00008B/816